Next Generation Physical Science and Everyday Thinking

Unit FM

Force-based Model for Interactions

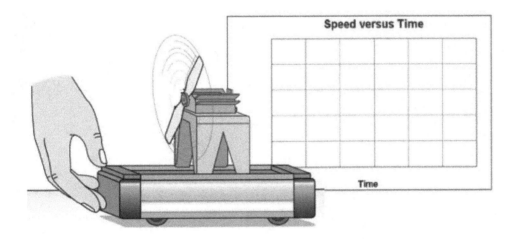

Next Gen

PETLC

Lecture-style Class

Next Generation Physical Science and Everyday Thinking

<u>Unit FM</u>
Force-based Model for Interactions

Lecture-style Class

Major support for the development of *Next Gen PET* **came from the National Science Foundation Grant No. 1044172 and the Chevron Corporation**

© 2018 San Diego State University Research Foundation

human energy·

Activate Learning
44 Amogerone Crossway #7862
Greenwich, CT 06836
www.activatelearning.com

Next Generation Physical Science and Everyday Thinking (*Next Gen PET*)
© 2018 San Diego State University Research Foundation
Licensed exclusively to Activate Learning.

Printed and bound in the United States of America.

ISBN 978-1-68231-335-0
6th Printing
6 7 8   22 21 20

This project was supported, in part, by the National
Science Foundation under Grant No. 1044172. Opinions
expressed are those of the authors and not necessarily those
of the National Science Foundation.

Next Gen PET Development Team

Co-authors of Next Gen PET

Fred Goldberg, San Diego State University
Stephen Robinson, Tennessee Technological University
Danielle Harlow, University of California at Santa Barbara
Julie Andrew, University of Colorado at Boulder
Edward Price, California State University at San Marcos
Michael McKean, San Diego State University

Contributed to Development of Materials

Valerie Otero, University of Colorado at Boulder
Paula Engelhardt, Tennessee Technological University
Rebecca Stober, University of Colorado at Boulder
Cary Sneider, Portland State University
Rebecca Kruse Vincent, National Science Foundation
Nephi Thompson, Colorado Mountain College
David Mitchell, California Polytechnic University at San Luis Obispo
Leslie Atkins, Boise State University

Field Test Collaborators

David Mitchell, California Polytechnic University at San Luis Obispo
Anne Marie Bergen, California Polytechnic University at San Luis Obispo
Lola Berber-Jimenez, California Polytechnic University at San Luis Obispo
Nancy Stauch, California Polytechnic University at San Luis Obispo
Tina Duran, California Polytechnic University at San Luis Obispo
Chance Hoellwarth, California Polytechnic University at San Luis Obispo
Paula Engelhardt, Tennessee Technological University

Technical Support

Shawn Alff, San Diego State University Katie
Badham, San Diego State University Megan
Santos, San Diego State University James
Powell, San Diego State University
Anne E. Leak, University of California at Santa Barbara
Noreen Balos, University of California at Santa Barbara
Leo Farias, California Polytechnic University at San Luis Obispo
Loren Johnson, California Polytechnic University at San Luis Obispo
Liz Walker, Tennessee Technological University
Ryan Calloway, Tennessee Technological University
Carla Moore, Tennessee Technological University
Ian Robinson, Tennessee Technological University
Rob Reab, Tennessee Technological University
Nate Reynolds, California State University at San Marcos
Lauran Gerhart, California State University at San Marcos

Unit FM: Force-based Model for Interactions
Table of Contents

Lesson #	Lesson (L) Title	Page
L1	**Interactions, Force, and Motion**	**FM-1**
Ext A[1]	Force Diagrams	*online*
L2	**Motion with a Continuous Force**	**FM-9**
Ext B	Pushing a Skateboarder	*online*
L3	**Pushes and Slowing Down**	**FM-15**
Ext C	Connecting Force and Energy Models	*online*
L4	**Forces and Friction**	**FM-21**
Ext D	How Does Friction Work?	*online*
L5	**Changing Force Strength and Mass**	**FM-27**
Ext E	Changing Direction	*online*
L6	**Falling Objects**	**FM-37**

UNIT FM

LESSON 1: Interactions, Force, and Motion

Purpose and Key Questions

When one object pushes or pulls on another object, scientists say it is exerting a *force*. All forces can be considered to be pushes or pulls. For example, when a soccer player kicks a ball, we say that the foot exerts a force on the ball. In this unit, we will be investigating the effects that forces have on the motion of objects.

We will start by examining how we can recognize when a force is acting on an object, and when it is not. In the example above, after the soccer player gets the ball moving with his kick (which is a quick push), is there still a force pushing the ball forward after the kick is over?

> **(1)** *When does the force of a quick push stop acting on an object?*
>
> **(2)** *When an object is moving, does this mean there must be a force pushing it in the direction of its motion?*

Predictions, Observations and Making Sense

Part 1. When does a force stop acting on an object?

To begin, watch a movie **(UFM L1 Movie 1)** of a person giving a cart a quick push to get it moving along a track. The cart and track are designed to minimize the effects of friction, so after the cart leaves the person's hand it moves along the rest of the track with very little slowing down.

 A speed-time graph for the cart is shown below. Discuss with your neighbors over what period on the graph you think the force caused by the hand is acting on the cart. Which labeled point on the graph is closest to your idea about when the force from the hand stops acting on the cart? Explain why you chose that particular point.

CQ 1-1: Which point on the graph is closest to where you think the force of the hand on the cart stopped acting on the cart?

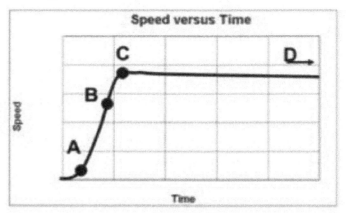

A. Point A
B. Point B
C. Point C
D. Not until he grabs it at the end of the track

Next, watch another movie **(UFM L1 Movie 2)**. In this case the cart will be given a gentle push to start it moving and then, while it is moving along the track, it will be given some more quick taps in the same direction as its motion.

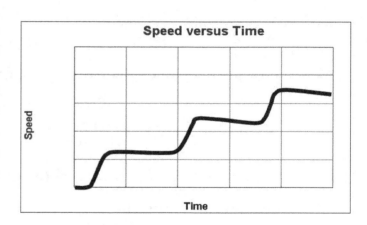

Its speed-time graph measured with a motion sensor should look similar to that shown above.

 Highlight the sections of the speed-time graph in which you think the hand was in contact with the cart. Why did you choose these sections?

When do you think the force caused by the hand is acting on the cart in this demonstration? Is it acting the whole time the cart is moving, or only during certain periods? Supposing you could measure the strength of this force while the cart is moving, which of the force-time graphs shown below best represents your thinking? Discuss this question with you neighbors and record your reasoning below.

CQ 1-2: Which force-time graph best represents your thinking about the force of the hand acting on the cart?

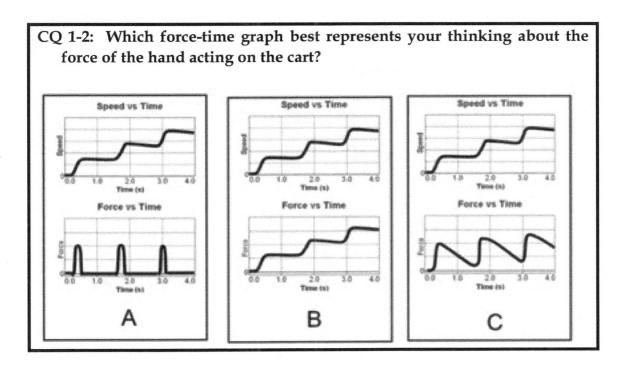

To check your thinking, watch a movie **(UFM L1 Movie 3)** of an experiment in which the strength of the force applied to the cart by the hand is measured, along with the speed.

 Which of the options in the question above most closely corresponds to the data recorded in the experiment?

Next, watch another movie **(UFM L1 Movie 4)**, this time from a computer simulation. Whenever the black arrow appears near the cart, that corresponds to when the cart is being pushed. The red arrow above the cart shows its relative speed. The duration of each push or force on the cart is longer than in the previous movie, so it is easier to see how the speed-time and force-time graphs are connected. Play the movie at least twice to see how the speed-time and force-time graphs are related.

Discuss the following questions with your group. Carefully compare the speed-time and force-time graphs from the two movies that you have just seen (displayed below). Remember that the *definition of force* is that it is *a push or a pull by one object on another*.

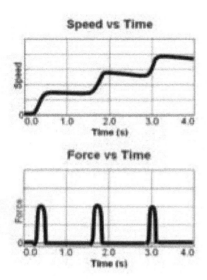
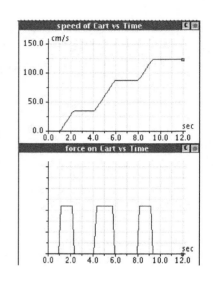

Did the hand exert a force on the cart the entire time it was moving, or only at certain times?

What happened to the speed of the cart while the hand was exerting a force on it? Did it increase quickly, decrease quickly, or remain reasonably constant?

What happened to the speed of the cart while the hand was **not** exerting a force on it? Did it increase quickly, decrease quickly, or remain reasonably constant?

According to the evidence from the graphs, did the force caused by the hand continue acting on the cart <u>after</u> it had lost contact with the cart? How do you know?

 Returning to CQ 1-1, which point on the speed-time graph is closest to where you think the force of the hand stopped acting on the cart?

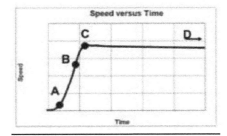

Part 2. If an object is moving, does that imply there must be a force acting on it in the direction of its motion?

Let us summarize what the class most likely agreed on in the previous part of the lesson.

- When the hand was pushing on the cart (in contact with it), the hand exerted a force on the cart.
- When the hand did not push on the cart, the hand did not exert a force on the cart.
- When the hand was exerting a force on the cart, the cart speeded up.
- When the hand was not exerting a force on the cart, the cart did not speed up, but instead moved at a (nearly) constant speed.

So, in deciding whether a force is or is not being exerted on a cart, evidence we can look for is whether the cart is speeding up or moving at constant speed.

Three students were considering the last movie you had just seen in the previous part of this lesson. They all agreed that while the hand is pushing the cart, there is a force acting on it, but had different ideas about whether a force is still pushing the cart forward after the hand has lost contact with it.

The force caused by the hand is transferred to the cart and is carried with it. That's why the cart keeps moving forward after the push.

The force of the hand stops when contact is lost, but some other force must be acting to keep the cart moving

After contact is lost there are no longer any forces pushing the cart forward. That's why it stops speeding up.

Samantha   Victor   Amara

 Discuss the students' ideas with your group, and then decide whom you agree with (if any).

CQ 1-3: In the discussion between three students about the force acting on the cart after the quick push, whom do you agree with?

a. Samantha
b. Victor
c. Amara
d. None of them

Part 3. Force, energy and transfer

In Unit EM you learned that during an interaction, energy is transferred from the giver to the receiver. Consider again the person giving the cart a quick shove with his hand. The person/hand and cart are interacting <u>only</u> during the short period of time when the hand is in contact with the cart. Below is a G/R energy diagram for just the interaction between the person/hand and the cart.

Contact push/pull interaction

Energy Giver

Energy Receiver

Person/Hand → Energy → Cart

Decrease in Chemical Potential Energy and Increase in Kinetic Energy

Increase in Kinetic Energy

The interaction occurs only during the period when the hand and cart are in contact, and it is only during that period that the speed of the cart changes from zero to some final value. It is also during that period that energy is transferred from the person/hand to the cart. As a consequence, the person/hand decreases in energy and the cart increases in energy (by the same amount). After the interaction is over, the person/hand continues with a smaller amount of energy, and the cart continues with a greater amount of energy, the difference being what was transferred. So the person/hand and the cart each have energy before the interaction, as well as after the interaction, but just different amounts.[1]

On the other hand, *a 'force' only exists during the interaction.* It does not exist before the interaction begins, and it does not exist after the interaction is over. Furthermore, a force always involves two objects—one object exerts a force on (interacts with) the other. A single object cannot interact with itself, and therefore an object cannot exert a force on itself.

---

[1] As analogy, think of transferring money from your checking account to your savings account. Before the transfer, each account has money. During the transfer, the checking account decreases in the amount of money it has and the savings account increases in the money it has. After the transfer, both the checking and savings accounts each have money, just a different amount (assuming you don't empty out your checking account).

Summarizing Questions

S1. Consider what quantity (or quantities) is (are) transferred during an interaction between two objects.

CQ 1-4: During a contact push/pull interaction between two objects, what do you think is <u>transferred</u> from one object to the other?

A. Energy
B. Force
C. Both energy and force
D. Neither energy nor force

Explain your reasoning.

S2. In addition to being able to look at a speed-time graph and infer something about the force acting on the object, you should also be able to look at a force-time graph and infer something about how the speed of the object is changing.

CQ 1-5: Suppose the force-time graph for a force acting on a certain object looked like this. Which of the speed-time graphs below **could** be produced by applying a single force in this way?

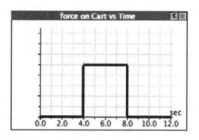

A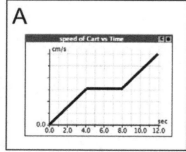

B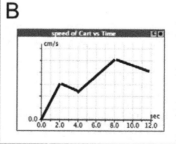

C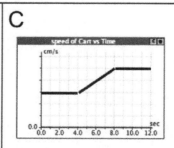

Purpose and Key Questions

In Lesson 1 you saw the effect that quick pushes had on the motion of a low-friction cart. This is like the situation in many sports, where the players move the ball (or puck) around using quick pushes of their hands, feet, or a bat/racket of some kind. Scientists call such quick pushes **impulsive** forces.

But what would the motion of an object be like if a single **continuous, constant** force acted on an object? By this, we mean a force that continues to act over a long time period and whose strength stays constant over that period. Thus, the force-time graph would like that shown to the right.

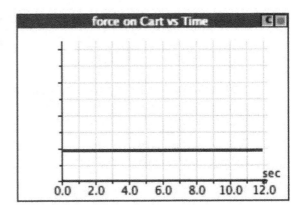

For example, suppose your friend was standing balanced on a skateboard and you pushed, and kept on pushing, with the same strength force, in the same direction. What would his motion be like?

How does an object move when a force of constant strength continuously pushes it forward?

Predictions, Observations and Making Sense

Imagine you had a low-friction cart at rest at one end of a track. Now, suppose you were to interact with the cart by pushing it continuously from behind with a **constant strength push.** What do you think its motion would be like? (With a low friction cart, we can assume the frictional effects are so small that we can ignore them.)

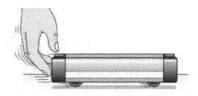

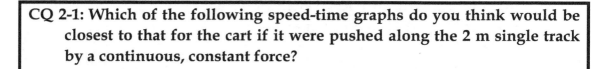 Discuss your thinking with your neighbors and decide which of the graphs in the question below best represents your thinking. Make a note of your reasoning below the question and then participate in the class vote and discussion.[1]

> **CQ 2-1: Which of the following speed-time graphs do you think would be closest to that for the cart if it were pushed along the 2 m single track by a continuous, constant force?**
>
>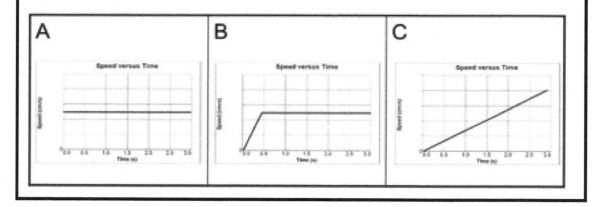

In order to test your thinking, we will need to find a way to apply a continuous, constant force to a cart. We will first try doing this by pushing manually, as we have before.

Watch a movie **(UFM L2 Movie 1)** of an experiment in which a person tries to use their hand to push a low-friction cart along a track using a continuous, constant force. The strength of the force the person is exerting on the cart will

---

[1] In real life, when you push an object, there is always some friction present which affects the motion. In this case, however, and in most examples for the next couple of lessons, we are ignoring the effects of friction.

be measured using a force probe attached to the cart, and the results will be displayed on a force-time graph.

 According to the force-time graph, was the force exerted on the cart continuous and constant? How can you tell?

In reality, most people find it very difficult to maintain a continuous push of a constant strength. We will now check to see if there is a better way to arrange for such a force to act on the cart.

Watch the movie **(UFM L2 Movie 2)** of a low-friction cart with a fan unit mounted on it. While the fan is running, the cart will push against the force probe, which will be held steady in front of it.

 Do you think the fan unit exerts a continuous, constant, force on the cart while it is running? What evidence supports your thinking??

Now that we have a way to apply a continuous, constant force to the cart, we can check how it moves when only this force is acting on it. Watch the movie **(UFM L2 Movie 3)** of an experiment in which a cart starts at rest and is pushed along a track by a fan unit. The speed-time graph of the cart will be displayed.

 Sketch the speed-time graph for the motion of the cart.

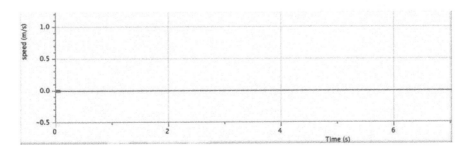

Discuss with your neighbors. What was happening to the speed of the cart while the fan unit was pushing it along the track? Does this confirm or refute your prediction from CQ 2-1?

Suppose this demonstration were repeated using three tracks joined end-to-end. Do you think the fan-cart would continue to speed up in this case, or do you think something else would happen?

CQ 2-2: If the fan-cart were started from rest and allowed to run along three tracks laid end-to-end, what do you think would happen?

A. Its speed would increase along the first track but become constant soon after that.
B. It would continue speeding up all the way along the three tracks.
C. It would speed up at first, and then begin to slow down.

To check your prediction, watch a movie **(UFM L2 Movie 4)** of the experiment being performed. The movie will be paused at the relevant points so that its time code can be used to estimate how long it takes the cart to travel the length of each of the three tracks.

 Record how long it takes for the fan-cart to travel down each of the three tracks,

First track:

Second track:

Third track:

 Discuss with your neighbors. What happens to the speed of the cart as it travels down the three tracks? Which of the responses to CQ 2-2 does the evidence from the movie support? Explain how you know.

Summarizing Questions

S1. If a low-friction cart is at rest and a force acts on it, what happens? If the same force continues to act on the cart, what happens to the cart's speed?

S2. In the previous lesson you saw that, just because an object is moving, this does not necessarily mean that a force is pushing it forward. So what evidence would you look for to tell you that there is definitely a force pushing it forward?

CQ 2-3: Which of the following would be <u>definite evidence</u> supporting the idea that a force is pushing an object <u>forward</u>?

A. Motion with decreasing speed only
B. Motion with increasing speed only
C. Motion with constant speed only
D. Any motion, regardless of how the speed is behaving

S3. Now consider what would happen if the fan blade jammed (and so suddenly stopped rotating) as the fan-cart was moving along the track.

CQ 2-4: Which of the following do you think would happen if the fan blade jammed (<u>stopped instantaneously</u>) as it was pushing the cart along the track?

A. It would continue speeding up until it reached the end of the track.
B. It would stop speeding up immediately.
C. It would continue to speed up for a short time.

Purpose and Key Questions

You have now seen evidence to support the idea that, when an object is moving, a single force applied to it in the same direction as its motion makes its speed increase. But what if the force is applied in the opposite direction to that in which the object is moving?

For example, suppose that while your friend is coasting along on his skateboard, you gave him a quick, gentle push in the opposite direction to that in which he was moving.

What do you think his motion would be like during your push? What about after your push?

Would something different happen if, instead of a quick push, you kept up a continuous constant push on your friend?

> 1. *What effect does a 'backward' push have on the motion of an object?*
>
> 2. *What happens if a continuous 'backward' push is applied to a moving object?*

Predictions, Observations and Making Sense

Part 1. Motion with quick backwards pushes.

Imagine a low-friction cart was moving along a track and someone gave it a **very gentle tap** with her hand *in the opposite direction to the direction it was moving*. What would its motion be like before, during, and after the push?

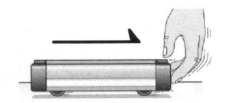

CQ 3-1: If a moving low friction cart were given a <u>very short, gentle, backwards tap</u>, which of the speed-time graphs below best represents what you think its motion would be like?

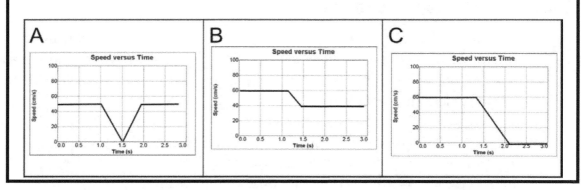

To check your thinking, watch a movie **(UFM L3 Movie 1)** of an experiment in which a moving cart will be given some gentle 'backward' taps as it moves along a track. The speed-time graph for the cart will be shown.

 What was the motion of the cart like during the short periods when the hand was applying a 'backwards' tap? Was it speeding up quickly, slowing down quickly, or moving at a reasonably constant speed? Why do you think it did this?

 In between the 'backward' taps, how does the cart appear to move? Does it appear to speed up significantly, slow down significantly, or move at a reasonably constant speed? Why do you think this is?

What forces do you think are acting on the cart during this demonstration? Recall that a force diagram shows the forces acting on, and the motion of, an object at a **particular moment in time**. What would force diagrams look like for three separate moments in time: *just before*, *during*, and *just after* one of the gentle 'backward' taps?

CQ 3-2: Which of the following series of force diagrams best represents your thinking about the forces acting on the cart before, during, and after a backward tap? (Assume all motion corresponds to times after the initial push.)

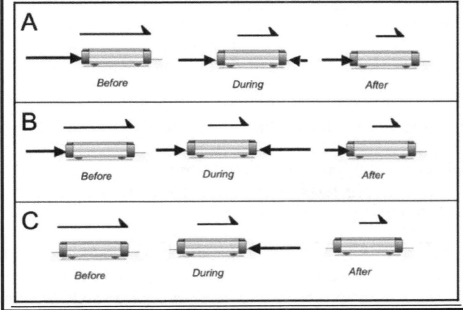

Next, watch a movie **(UFM L3 Movie 2)** of a simulation of a moving cart being given some gentle 'backward' taps as it moves along a track. Both the speed-time and force-time graphs for the cart will be shown.

Sketch the speed-time and force-time graphs for the simulator cart.

Mark the short periods on both graphs where a 'backward' tap was applied. Explain how you knew which sections of the graph to mark.

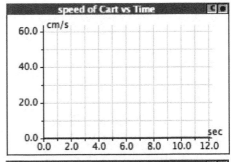

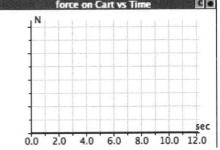

What happens to the cart's speed during the 'backward' taps? What about between the taps?

 Does a force act on the cart during the 'backward' taps? What about between the taps? How do you know?

Part 2. Motion with a continuous backwards force

Now suppose, instead of applying gentle 'backwards' taps, a fan unit was used to exert a <u>continuous</u> force on a cart that is initially in the opposite direction to its motion.

CQ 3-3: Imagine a low friction cart initially moving to the right (after an initial shove) had a continuous force pushing to the left on it. Which of the speed-time graphs below best represents what you think its motion would be like?

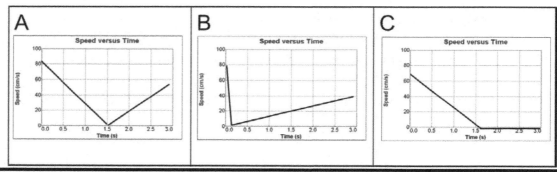

To check your prediction, watch a movie **(UFM L3 Movie 3)** of an experiment in which a cart with a fan unit attached is given a quick push to start it moving in such a way that the fan exerts a force that is initially in the **opposite direction to the cart's motion**. You should focus your attention on the portion of the speed-time graph that shows the cart's motion after the initial push.

 Which of the choices in CQ 3-3 best represents the real cart's motion after the initial push?

While the cart was moving **away** from its starting position (**after** the initial push), was it speeding up, slowing down, or moving at a reasonably constant speed? Why do you think this was?

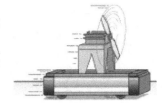

 While the cart was moving back **toward** its starting position, was it speeding up, slowing down, or moving at a reasonably constant speed? Why did the manner in which the cart was moving change?

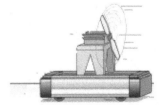

Summarizing Questions

S1. Consider the force diagrams shown below and decide what the motion of these two carts would be like.

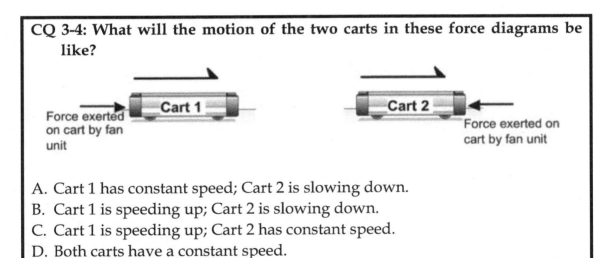

CQ 3-4: What will the motion of the two carts in these force diagrams be like?

A. Cart 1 has constant speed; Cart 2 is slowing down.
B. Cart 1 is speeding up; Cart 2 is slowing down.
C. Cart 1 is speeding up; Cart 2 has constant speed.
D. Both carts have a constant speed.

S2. You have now seen evidence of how an object moves when a single force acts on it, either pushing it in the same direction as its motion or pushing on it in the opposite direction to its motion. What do both of these situations have in common, in terms of how they affect the motion of the object?

UNIT FM
LESSON 4: Forces and Friction

Purpose and Key Questions

In the previous lesson, you saw that when a force is exerted on a moving object in a direction opposite to that of its motion, the object slows down. Is such a force always responsible when things slow and stop, or would a moving object eventually slow and stop on its own?

In the experiments you have seen in previous lessons, you may have noticed that, providing no force was pushing them forward, the carts being used slowed down gradually, even when there was not a hand or a fan unit pushing them 'backwards'. For example, this speed-time graph shows a cart slowing down gradually after being given a quick push to start it moving.

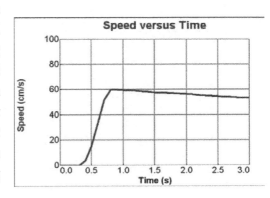

As you saw in Unit EM, we can attribute this behavior to the effects of friction. But when this happens, is a force acting on the cart just like it did when a fan or hand was used to slow it down? Or is a force not involved and slowing down is just something that happens to all moving objects naturally?

1. Is friction a force?

2. If so, in what direction does it act?

Predictions, Observations and Making Sense

Four students are discussing a demonstration in which someone gave a cart a quick push and then let it move along the track on its own.

They have noticed that the speed-time graph on the previous page indicates that the cart was slowing down very gradually after the initial push, and discuss why they think this was happening. They have also drawn force diagrams of the cart after the initial push to show their ideas. Working by yourself (not with your group), decide which of the students' ideas makes the most sense to you and vote accordingly.

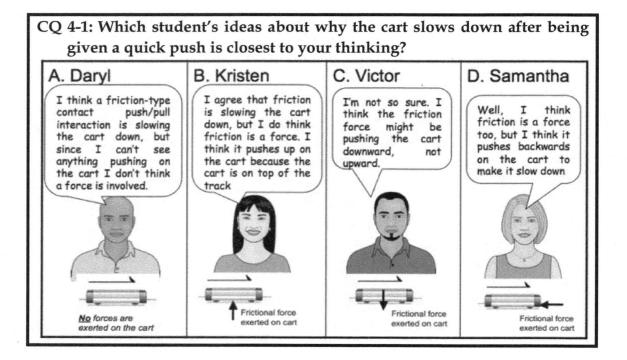

CQ 4-1: Which student's ideas about why the cart slows down after being given a quick push is closest to your thinking?

A. Daryl
I think a friction-type contact push/pull interaction is slowing the cart down, but since I can't see anything pushing on the cart I don't think a force is involved.

No forces are exerted on the cart

B. Kristen
I agree that friction is slowing the cart down, but I do think friction is a force. I think it pushes up on the cart because the cart is on top of the track

Frictional force exerted on cart

C. Victor
I'm not so sure. I think the friction force might be pushing the cart downward, not upward.

Frictional force exerted on cart

D. Samantha
Well, I think friction is a force too, but I think it pushes backwards on the cart to make it slow down

Frictional force exerted on cart

Now discuss the four students' ideas with other members of your group and decide which student's idea now makes the most sense to you.

We will now consider some experiments that can help decide which of the student's reasoning is consistent with the evidence.

In the previous lesson, you saw how a fan unit could be used to make a cart slow down after it is given a quick shove to start it moving. Watch the movie **(UFM L4 Movie 1)** of this experiment again.

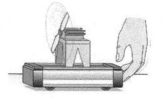

Sketch the speed-time graph for the motion of the cart below and label it 'FAN'.

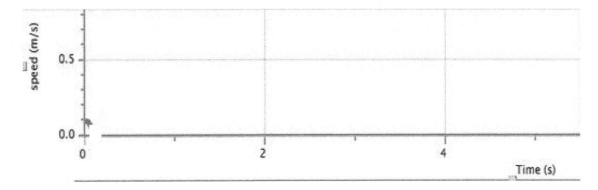

 What evidence does this graph provide that, **after the initial push**, a force was acting on the cart in a direction opposite its motion? What force was this?

 Complete the force diagram for this cart for a moment in time during the period it was slowing down, **after the initial push**. Be sure to label any force arrows you draw.

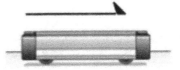

Next watch a movie **(UFM L4 Movie 2)** of an experiment involving a similar cart that has a 'friction pad' attached. This pad will be lowered so that the pad will rub on the track as the cart moves along the track.

Upside down Low-friction cart

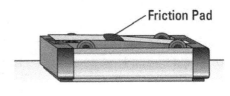

Friction Pad

Just as in the previous experiment, the friction-cart will be given a quick push to start it moving along the track and then left to slow and stop on its own.

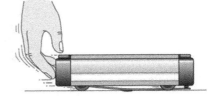

Use a different color to sketch the speed-time graph on the same set of axes you used on the previous page. Label the graph 'FRICTION'.

 After the initial push has ended, how does the motion of the cart with the friction pad lowered compare with the motion of the cart with the fan unit pushing 'backward' on it? Are the motions reasonably similar, or are they very different? (Focus on the general shape of the graphs, not small details.)

 If your speed-time graphs were not labeled, would it be possible for someone who did not see the experiments to tell which one was produced using the fan unit to slow the cart, and which was produced using the friction pad?

 Discuss with your neighbors what a comparison between the results of these two experiments implies about whether friction is or is not a force. Discuss which of the ideas in the following question you think is supported by the evidence you have seen.[1]

CQ 4-2: Which of the following ideas about friction does a comparison between the results of these two demonstrations support?

A. Friction is not a force.
B. Friction is a force that pushes backward on a moving object.
C. Friction is a force that pushes upward on a moving object.
D. Friction is a force that pushes downward on a moving object.

---

[1] You may be wondering how it is that two surfaces rubbing together could produce a force in the direction implied by the results of these demonstrations. This will be the subject of the homework assignment that follows this lesson, in which you will consider a model that may help you think about this issue.

Summarizing Questions

S1. In this lesson you saw how a cart with a friction pad slowed down, but even without this attachment a cart will slow down gradually. How could you illustrate this difference using force diagrams? Consider the following question and make a note of your reasoning.

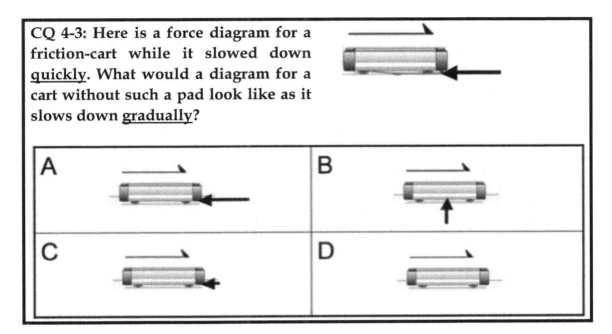

CQ 4-3: Here is a force diagram for a friction-cart while it slowed down **quickly**. What would a diagram for a cart without such a pad look like as it slows down **gradually**?

A

B

C

D

S2. Maglev (magnetic-levitation) trains use powerful magnets to lift the train a short distance above its track, thus eliminating any frictional forces between them. However, if the force that is pushing it forward were to disappear, such a maglev train would still gradually slow down and stop.

What else do you think the train is interacting with that would exert a force on it in the opposite direction to its motion, thus tending to make it slow down?

S3. How do you think an object would move if you could arrange for absolutely **no forces** to act on it? For example, suppose a spacecraft is at rest in deep space so that **no form of friction or gravity is acting on it**. The main engine is fired for a few seconds (to start it moving) and is then shut off. Consider the following question about this situation and make a note of your reasoning.

CQ 4-4: A spacecraft fires its engine for a few seconds to start it moving. What do you think the motion of the spacecraft would be like <u>after</u> the engine is shut off so that <u>no forces</u> act on it?

A. It would continue to speed up for a while and then move at a constant speed.
B. It would move at a constant speed.
C. It would immediately begin to slow down.
D. It would continue to speed up for a while and then begin to slow down.

Purpose and Key Question

You now know that when a single force acts on an object, its speed changes, increasing or decreasing, depending on whether the force acts in the same direction as its motion or opposite to it. But how do the strength of the force and the mass of the object affect the manner in which the speed changes? For example, if you were to continuously push your friend on his well-oiled skateboard, how would his motion change (if at all) if you pushed harder? Would it also make a difference if he were carrying a backpack full of books, so increasing the mass you have to push?

 When a single force acts on an object, how is the object's motion affected by 1) the strength of that force and 2) the object's mass?

Predictions, Observations and Making Sense

Part 1. The effects of force strength

You have seen that a fan unit can be used to increase or decrease the speed of a low-friction cart, depending on whether it is pushing in the same direction as, or opposite to, the cart's direction of motion. Suppose you used a stronger fan unit in either of these situations. How do you think the motion of the cart would be different, if at all?

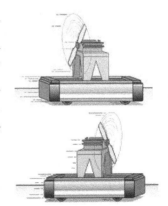

CQ 5-1: How would a fan cart's motion be different (if at all) if a <u>stronger fan</u> were used to speed it up or slow it down?

A. Its speed would both increase and decrease at a slower rate.
B. Its speed would both increase and decrease at a faster rate.
C. Its speed would increase and decrease at the same rate as when a weaker fan was used.
D. Its speed would increase at a faster rate, but decrease at a slower rate.

In order to test your thinking, we will need to find a way to vary the strength of the fan's pushes on the cart. In the past, it has been suggested that using a different number of batteries to power the fan unit might be a way of doing this.

Watch a movie **(UFM L5 Movie 1)** of an experiment involving a low-friction cart with a fan unit mounted on it. The force strength with which the fan-cart pushes against a force probe will be measured with different numbers of batteries installed in the fan unit.

 Does the evidence in the movie suggest that changing the number of batteries powering the fan unit changes the strength of the force with which it pushes on the cart?

Next, watch a movie **(UFM L5 Movie 2)** of an experiment in which a cart (starting at rest) is pushed along a track with different force strengths. The speed-time graphs corresponding to the different force strengths will be displayed.

 Sketch the speed-time graphs for the motion of the cart. Label the lines that correspond to the weaker and stronger force strengths.

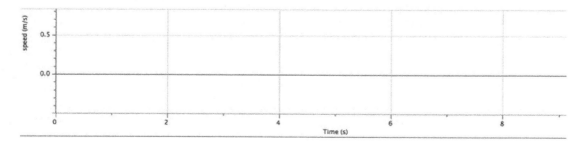

What is different about how the speed of the cart behaves when different strength forces act on it in the same direction as its motion? How does the speed-time graph show this difference?[1]

 Is this result what you expected?

Next, watch a movie **(UFM L5 Movie 3)** of an experiment in which different strength fan units are used to *slow* a cart (after an initial push). Speed-time graphs corresponding to the different force strengths will be displayed.

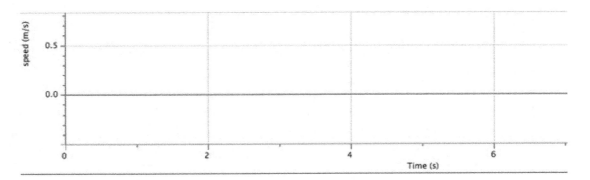

Sketch the speed-time graphs for the motion of the cart(s). Label which lines correspond to the weaker and stronger force strengths.

 What is different about how the speed of the cart behaves **after the initial push** when different strength 'backward' forces are acting on it? How does the speed-time graph show this difference?

 In the first experiment, you saw that increasing the strength of the force resulted in the cart's speed changing (in this case increasing) at a faster rate. In the second experiment, when a stronger force was used to slow

---

[1] The slope of the speed-time graph corresponds to the rate of change of speed with time. Thus, a greater positive slope on the speed-time graph means the cart is speeding up at a greater rate.

the cart, did its speed also change at a faster rate, or did it change at a slower rate? Explain how you know.

Part 2. The effects of mass

Having now investigated how force strength affects the motion of an object, we will now move on to investigate how the mass of an object affects its motion when a single force acts on it. However, before doing this, we must make sure we understand what scientists mean by *mass* and how it is different from *weight*.

> *<u>Mass</u> is a measure of the amount of matter an object is made of. The mass of a given object is the same no matter where in the universe it is. Mass is measured in kilograms (kg). <u>Weight</u> is a measure of the pull of a planet's gravity on an object. The weight of a given object will change depending where in the universe it is. Weight is measured in newtons (N).*
>
> *As an example of the difference, if you stood on the surface of the Moon, your mass would be exactly the same as it is here on Earth. However, your weight would be much less because the Moon's gravity is much weaker than Earth's.*

Now, imagine two identical fan-carts were started side-by-side on two tracks, and had a race.

 If the race ended in a tie, what could you infer about the relative strengths of the forces exerted by the two fan units?

Next, suppose some extra mass was added to one of the carts so that its total mass was now three times that of the other cart.

 Do you think the race would still end in a tie? Why, or why not? Explain your reasoning.

To test your thinking, watch a movie **(UFM L5 Movie 4)** of an experiment in which carts with different masses start at rest and are pushed along a track with fans of the same force strength. The speed-time graphs corresponding to the different masses will be displayed.

 Sketch the speed-time graphs for the motion of the two cart(s). Label which line corresponds to the cart with more mass and which line to the cart with less mass.

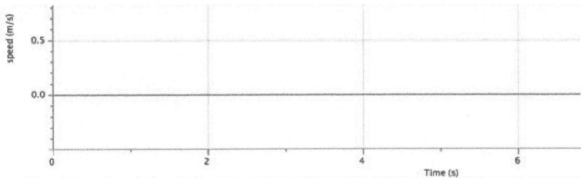

 When the same strength force acted to speed up the two carts, which cart's speed increased at a faster rate, the one with less mass or the one with more mass?

 Was the result of the race what you expected?

Now, suppose that instead of using the fan units to push two carts along a track, the carts were given a quick push to get them moving and then the fan units pushed on them in the opposite direction to their motion to slow them down. How do you think the different masses of the carts would affect how they slowed down after the initial push, assuming the initial pushes got them **started moving at about the same speed** and the fans pushed 'backward' with the same force strength?

Which of the two carts do you think would be the first to slow to a stop and reverse direction? Discuss the following clicker question with your group and decide on the answer that makes the most sense to you.

CQ 5-2: When the same strength <u>backward force</u> acts on two carts with different masses that are initially moving at the same speed, which cart do you think will slow to a stop and reverse direction first?

A.   The cart with more mass.
B.   Both carts will slow and stop together.
C.   The cart with less mass.

To test your prediction, watch the movie **(UFM L5 Movie 5)** in which two carts of different mass, and with the same strength fan pushing backward on them, are given a quick push to get them moving at about the same speed.

 Which cart slows to a stop first, the one with less mass or the one with more mass? Does this observation agree with your prediction?

 When the same strength force acted to slow down the two carts, which cart slowed down at a faster rate, the one with less mass or the one with more mass? How do you know?

 After they changed direction, the carts headed back toward their starting positions, speeding up as they went. Which cart sped up at the higher rate, the one with more mass or the one with less mass?

 Suppose the motions of these two carts were measured using a motion sensor. What would the speed-time graphs of the two carts look like? Choose from the possible graphs in the following clicker question,

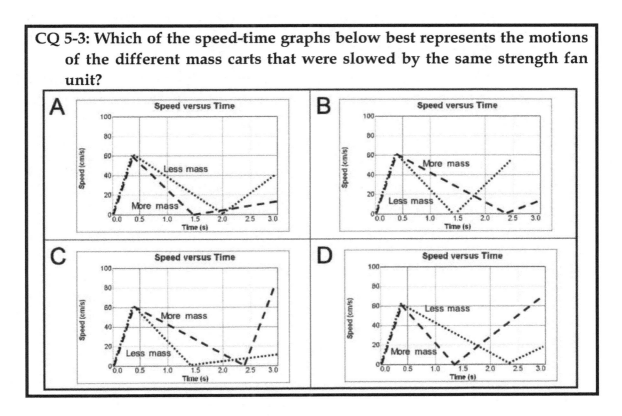

CQ 5-3: Which of the speed-time graphs below best represents the motions of the different mass carts that were slowed by the same strength fan unit?

Part 3. Combining the effects of both force strength and mass

Let's consider a race between two carts. One cart has a total mass of 6 kg while the other had a mass of only 2 kg. The same strength fan force of 20 N acts on each of them. Watch a movie **(UFM L5 Movie 6)** from a computer simulation of this situation.

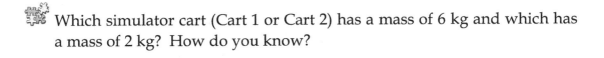 Which simulator cart (Cart 1 or Cart 2) has a mass of 6 kg and which has a mass of 2 kg? How do you know?

To make both carts increase speed at the same rate, and hence make the race a tie, what strength force should the fan acting on the 6 kg cart push with? (Remember, its mass is three times greater than the lighter cart.) Explain your reasoning.

In a moment you will watch a movie **(UFM L5 Movie 7)** in which the simulation will be run four times. Each time the strength of the fan force being applied to the 6 kg cart will be set to a different value: 10 N, 40 N, 60 N and 80N. The force strength on the 2 kg cart will be kept at 20 N throughout. Before viewing the movie, discuss with your group members what you predict you will see happening in the movies.

 For which value of the force strength on the 6 kg cart does the race between the two carts end in a tie? Does this agree with your prediction above?

Summarizing Questions

S1. To the right is a speed-time graph for a cart that was given a quick push along the track and then gradually slowed down. Which force do you think was stronger, the initial push or the one that slowed it down? How do you know?

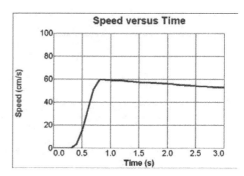

S2: In Parts 1 and 2 of this lesson you considered mostly cases in which you compared the motion of two objects for which only the force strength **or** the mass was different. But what if you had two objects that both had **different masses** and were acted on by forces of **different strengths**? How could you predict which object's speed would change at a faster rate under these circumstances?

Two students, Amara and Han, were discussing their ideas about a relationship that they could use to help them decide:

> *Amara: We saw that the greater the force strength, the faster the speed changes. I also think that the more mass an object has, the faster it slows down, so increases in the force strength and mass both produce a faster change in speed. That makes me think the rate at which the speed of an object changes depends on the force strength multiplied by the mass.*
> *Han: I agree with what you say about the force strength, but the speed of the cart with more mass increased at a slower rate, not a faster one. I think you have to divide the force strength by the mass to find out about the rate at which the speed will change.*

In terms of a mathematical relationship, Amara thinks:

Rate of change in speed = Strength of force × Mass of object,

while Han thinks:

$$\textbf{Rate of change in speed} = \frac{\textbf{Strength of force}}{\textbf{Mass of object}}$$

CQ 5-4. Do you agree with Amara, Han, or neither of them?

A. Amara
B. Han
C. Neither of them

Explain your reasoning.

S3: Some students have a race between two different fan carts. Cart A has a mass of 0.5 kg and a fan strength of 0.3 N. Cart B has a mass of 0.7 kg and a fan strength of 0.4 N.

CQ 5-5. Which cart will win the race?[2] Explain why.

A. Cart A
B. Cart B
C. They will end in a tie.

---

[2] When the force strength is measured in units of newtons (N) and the mass is measured in kilograms (kg), the units of 'rate of change of speed' will be *(meters per second) per second* [(m/s)/s]. These units tell us how quickly the speed (in m/s) will change during one second. For example a 'rate of change of speed' of 5 (m/s)/s means the speed will change by 5 m/s for every second that the force is being applied.

Newton's Second Law

In this lesson, the evidence suggested that when a **single force** acts on an object, the rate at which its speed changes can be found by using the relationship:

$$Rate\ of\ change\ in\ speed = \frac{Strength\ of\ force}{Mass\ of\ object}$$

Since this relationship can describe the motion of an object (in terms of its rate of change in speed), assuming both the force strength and its mass are known, it represents a mathematical model. The mathematical model was first developed by Sir Isaac Newton in the 17th century and is one form of what has since come to be known as *Newton's Second Law of Motion*. In the next unit, we will consider situations in which more than one force acts on an object at the same time and will learn how to revise this model to account for the more complex situation.

Purpose and Key Question

In the previous lessons, you developed your ideas about how the motion of an object is related to the forces acting on it using objects that move horizontally. However, it can be shown that exactly the same ideas can be applied to objects that move vertically (up and down). You know that if you hold an object up and then release it, it will fall to the floor. In this lesson, you will explore how different objects fall and, in particular, how their mass affects how they fall. You will also consider how the results can be explained using your ideas about forces.[1]

How does the mass of an object affect how it falls?

Predictions, Observations and Making Sense

Part 1. Describing falling objects[2]

> **CQ 6-1:** Hold a pencil above your desk, then release it and let it fall. While it was falling, what do you think the motion of the pencil was like? Choose the speed-time graph that best represents the motion.
>
>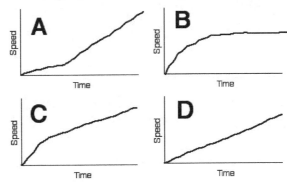

---

[1] Throughout this lesson we will assume that the effects of the force that the air exerts on falling objects, called the drag force, is negligible, and can be ignored. You will explore the drag force in an extension in the next unit.

[2] If you have worked through UPEF L4 you can skip all but the last question in Part 1.

Watch a movie **(UFM L6 Movie 1)** of a falling ball. A speed-time graph is also displayed.

 Describe what happens to the ball **after** it is let go.

 Sketch the speed-time graph below.

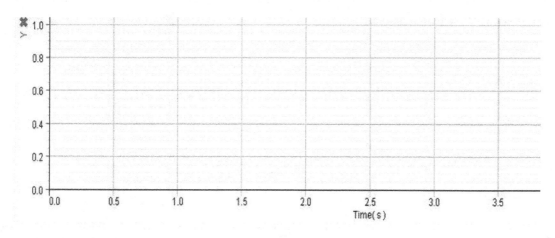

Time(s)

Do you think that a force was acting on the ball **while it was falling**? If so, how does the speed-time graph support your answer? If not, then why not?

If you think there is a force acting on the ball, what other **object** is exerting the force on the ball?

To the right is a drawing of a ball. Draw a motion arrow, and draw and label a force arrow representing the force acting on the ball as it falls.

You have learned that Newton's Second Law of Motion describes how the rate of change of speed of an object depends on both the net force acting on the object and the mass of the object.

$$Rate\ of\ change\ in\ speed = \frac{Strength\ of\ force}{Mass\ of\ object}$$

Although you applied this mathematical model exclusively to describe objects moving horizontally, it is a very general model and can also be used to describe objects moving in any direction subject to any types of forces.

Part 2. How does mass affect the falling motion of objects?

Imagine you were to hold two spheres of a similar size, but different mass, at the same height above the ground and released them at the same time.

 Which sphere do you think would hit the ground first (if either) and why? Discuss this with your group and choose the option in the clicker question that is closest to your thinking.

> **CQ 6-2: Suppose you were to drop two spheres of similar sizes, but different masses, from the same height at the same time. Which would reach the ground first, and why?**
>
> A. Both would reach the ground at the same time because the forces acting on them have different strengths.
> B. The more massive sphere would reach the ground first because it has a stronger force acting on it.
> C. The less massive sphere would reach the ground first because the forces acting the balls have the same strength.
> D. Both would reach the ground at the same time because the forces acting on them have the same strength.
> E. Some other result or reasoning—you describe it.

We will begin collecting evidence to support one of the answers in the clicker question by first considering which ball would hit the ground first, if either. Watch a movie **(UCF L6 Movie 2)** of a demonstration in which several spheres of the same size, but different masses, are dropped onto a board in pairs to see if there is pattern to how they fall.

 When two spheres are dropped, does the more massive one or the less massive one clearly hit the board first, or do they both appear to hit at the same time?

 Based on your observations, does the mass of an object seem to affect the rate at which its speed increases as it falls? What evidence supports your conclusion?

Part 3. How does the strength of the gravitational force on an object depend on its mass?

Having now seen how objects with different masses fall, we will next consider how the strengths of the gravitational forces acting on them compare.

First, pick up a fairly massive object (e.g. a backpack) and hold it out in front of you palms up for a few seconds. You can feel the strength of the force that you have to push upwards with your hand in order to keep the object motionless. While you are pushing up on the object, at the same time the Earth is also pulling down on that object — that is the gravitational force. You know this because if you were to let go, the object would fall to the ground due to just the gravitational force.

> **CQ 6-3: While you are holding the object <u>steady</u>, how does the strength of the force that you need to push upward on the object compare to the strength of the gravitational force that the Earth is pulling down on the object?**
>
> A. Your upward force is stronger than the Earth's downward force.
> B. Your upward force is weaker than the Earth's downward force.
> C. Your upward force is equal in strength to the Earth's downward force.

Next, pick up a less massive object (e.g., a cell phone) to hold in the other hand, palms up. Hold both objects out in front of you for several seconds. Consider the strengths of the forces that your two hands are exerting upward to keep the two objects motionless.

 Is the strength of your hand's upward force on the much more massive object stronger than, weaker than, or the same strength as the upward force your other hand is exerting on the less massive object? Why do you think so?

To have a concrete example that everyone can refer to, imagine that you were holding two different carts in your hands. The 2-kg cart would be the less massive object, and the 6-kg cart would be the more massive object.

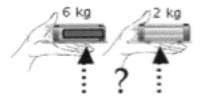

Based on the previous class discussion, you know that the Earth is also exerting a gravitational force downward on each of the two objects.

CQ 6-4: While the 6 kg and 2 kg carts are being held up, how do you think the strength of the gravitational forces pulling downward on the two carts compare?

A. A stronger gravitational force acts on the 6 kg cart.
B. The same strength gravitational force acts on both carts.
C. A stronger gravitational force acts on the 2 kg cart.

Following the class discussion about the clicker question, fill in the following according to what makes the most sense to you.

> *The Earth exerts a* _____ *(different, same) strength gravitational force on objects with different masses. The strength of the Earth's gravitational force is* _____ *(greater, weaker, the same) on a more massive object than on a less massive object.*

Part 4. How can objects of different masses all fall at the same rate of increase in speed?

In Part 2 of this lesson, you saw evidence to support the idea that objects with different masses all fall at the **same** rate of increasing speed (assuming the effects of air drag are negligible). However, in Part 3 you considered a simple situation that supports the idea that the strength of the gravitational force exerted on objects by the Earth is **different**, depending on the object's mass. How can it be that objects of different masses, with different strength gravitational forces acting on them, all fall at the same rate of increasing speed? To help you think about this issue, consider a race between two carts of different masses (traveling horizontally).

Imagine you had a race between two low-friction fan-carts along side-by-side tracks, like those shown here. These carts have **different masses** (6 kg and 2 kg), but the **same strength force** (20 N) acts on each of them.

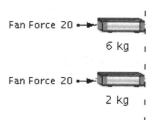

 Would this race end in a tie? If so, why? If not, why not, and how could you make it end in a tie? Discuss the question below and choose the option that is closest to your thinking, while also making a note of your reasoning. If you chose option A or B, also propose new values for force strengths that would make the race end in a tie.

CQ 6-5: What, if anything, would you need to do to make the race between the 6 kg and 2 kg carts end in a tie?

A. Increase the strength of the force acting on the force acting on the 6 kg cart. (Indicate what its new value should be.)
B. Increase the strength of the force acting on the 2 kg cart. (Indicate what its new value should be.)
C. Do nothing; the race will end in a tie with the forces as they are.

Watch a movie **(UFM L6 Movie 3)** of the race being run on the simulator with a 60 N force acting on the 6-kg cart. A 20 N force acts on the 2-kg cart.

What force strength acting on the 6-kg cart made the race end in a tie? Why do you think this value works?

 We know that Newton's Second Law can be used to explain why two carts of different masses and forces on them can race to a tie. Now consider two falling objects with different masses. You know they fall together (their 'race' downward is a tie), so what does that mean for the relative strengths of the gravitational forces acting on objects of different masses?

Summarizing Questions

S1. The results from Part 2 suggest that if the 6 kg and 2 kg carts were dropped from the same height at the same time, they would reach the ground together. How could you explain such a result in terms of the relative strengths of the gravitational forces pulling the carts downward? Discuss this and choose the option in the question below that corresponds to your thinking.

CQ 6-6: Which of the following ideas would explain the fact that the 6 kg and 2 kg carts would reach the ground at the same time?

A. That the force pulling the 2 kg cart downward is three times stronger than that pulling on the 6 kg cart.

B. That the forces pulling both carts downward have the same strength.

C. That the force pulling the 6 kg cart downward is three times stronger than that pulling on the 2 kg car.

S2. Imagine a soccer ball and a much more massive bowling ball being dropped at the same time from the same height above the ground.

CQ 6-7: Which of these force diagrams best represents the gravitational forces acting on a soccer ball and bowling ball as they fall?

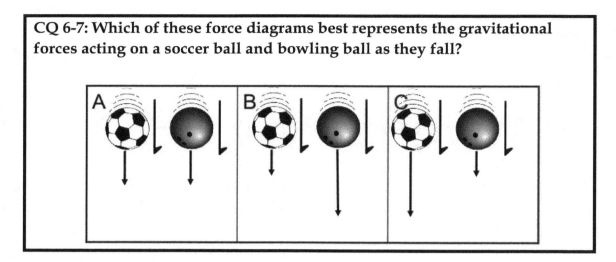

ISBN 978-1-68231-335-0